WHAT IS A THOUGHT?

> THOUGHTS ARE BALLOONS IN THE HEAD.
> — Peter, 5

> A THOUGHT IS WHEN SOMETHING YOU THINK IN YOUR BRAIN POPS IN YOUR MIND.
> — Yasmin, 7

> THOUGHTS ARE WHEN YOU THINK AND THEN YOU HAVE AN IDEA AND YOU THINK ABOUT IT IN YOUR HEAD.
> — Zoravar, 8

> IT'S LIKE A PICTURE IN YOUR HEAD WHEN YOU TRY TO COPY OR SOMETHING, WHEN YOU'RE PAINTING.
> — Sophia, 5

> A THOUGHT IS WHEN YOU HAVE TO GO SOMEWHERE ELSE WITH SOMEONE YOU LIKE.
> — Theo, 4

> THEY ARE GOOD IDEAS THAT YOU THINK, USEFUL THINGS TO HELP, IDEAS THAT HELP YOU DO STUFF. IF YOU DIDN'T HAVE THOUGHTS, LIFE WOULD BE BORING!
> — Morgane, 8

> IT'S BRAINS, IT'S THE MIND THINKING IN MEMORIES, IDEAS AND REMEMBERING THINGS.
> — Stanley, 6

> A THOUGHT IS WHEN SOMEONE TELLS YOU SOMETHING AND IT GOES INTO YOUR BRAIN.
> — Jaś, 7

> IT'S TOAST AND EARRINGS …!!!
> — Douglas, 4

I THINK I CAN'T SLEEP

To my three favourite thinkers:

J R M

WRITTEN BY
ANNA KAMINSKI

Text copyright ©Anna Kaminski 2017. Illustrations copyright ©Martinus van Tee 2017. Published by Anna Kaminski, 2017. All rights reserved.
ISBN-10: 1981318984 | ISBN-13: 978-1981318988
Thank you Casey D'Entremont for your encouragement and editing this book for me.

I love passing by, in and out,
on and off, up and down.

I wax and wane.
I float and I bounce.

I invade and withdraw.
Being still just isn't my thing.

Sometimes what we do creates **CHAOS** in (your) mind.

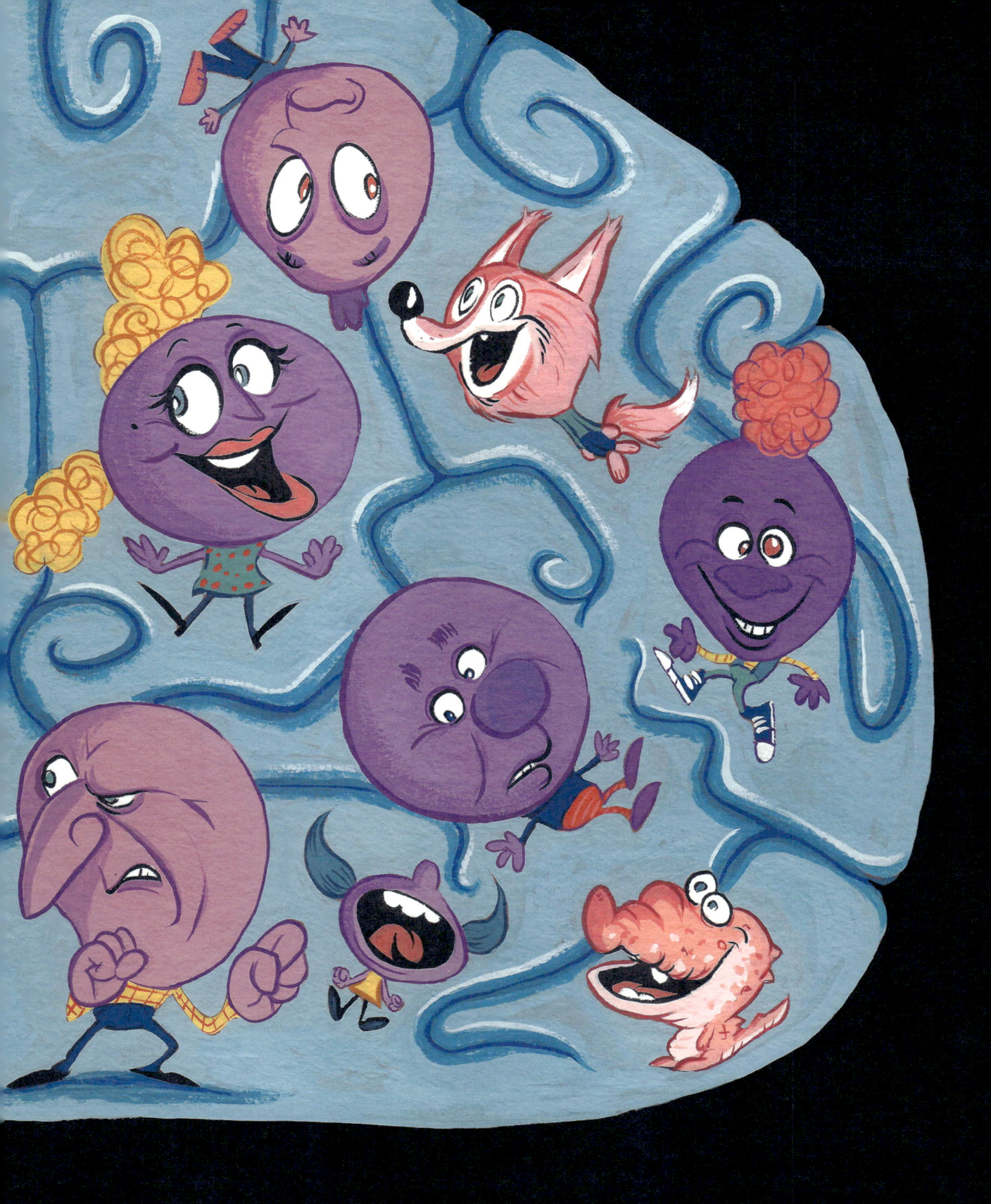

Take **ADAM**.

Adam is a boy whose birthday is tomorrow. He loves his birthdays and thinks (that's us, **THOUGHTS!**) that they are better than Christmases.

ADAM SAYS:

Sure, you get presents at Christmas, too. There are treats and parties. But **YOUR** birthday is **ONLY YOURS**: friends come **ESPECIALLY** to **CELEBRATE YOU**.
The cake to eat, and the candles to blow, and wishes to make, and balloons to pop are all **FOR YOU**.

Adam is so excited that he just can't sleep.
Has this ever happened to you?

I can't wait! Still the whole night, I wish it was tomorrow! Will anyone come to my party? What if they don't? They came to Tommy's birthday, I loved that party, super cool balloons. Did mum remember to buy the **RED BALLOONS**? I love red, it's actually my favourite. When I was 4 I liked blue but everyone else did so I picked another colour. Now it's just me and Amy who likes red. Amy borrowed a book from me yesterday. She likes red and **PIRATES**. The book was about pirates and lots of blood. I'm turning 8; it will be awesome to be 8. I'm the tallest in the class; I look 10. My school shirt is size 10. Tom is the small

...arrived. I've never been to the **HOSPITAL** and thought it would be cool to go see all the machines and beds going up and down. I feel bad about hoping that someone goes to hospital! Ms. Kim at school says it's not nice to wish bad things on people. I do sometimes, but I don't tell anyone. Oh it's **SO LATE** and I just can't sleep! Just like before the holidays last year... We were getting on the bus the next morning and I hate buses. Sure enough I was sick during that trip. Mum wasn't impressed! There was another boy vomiting into a plastic bag in the row next to us. **YUK!** ...in the class. He missed school last week. We all secretly hoped he was sick and we could visit him at the hospital but he wasn't. His **GRANDMOTHER**...

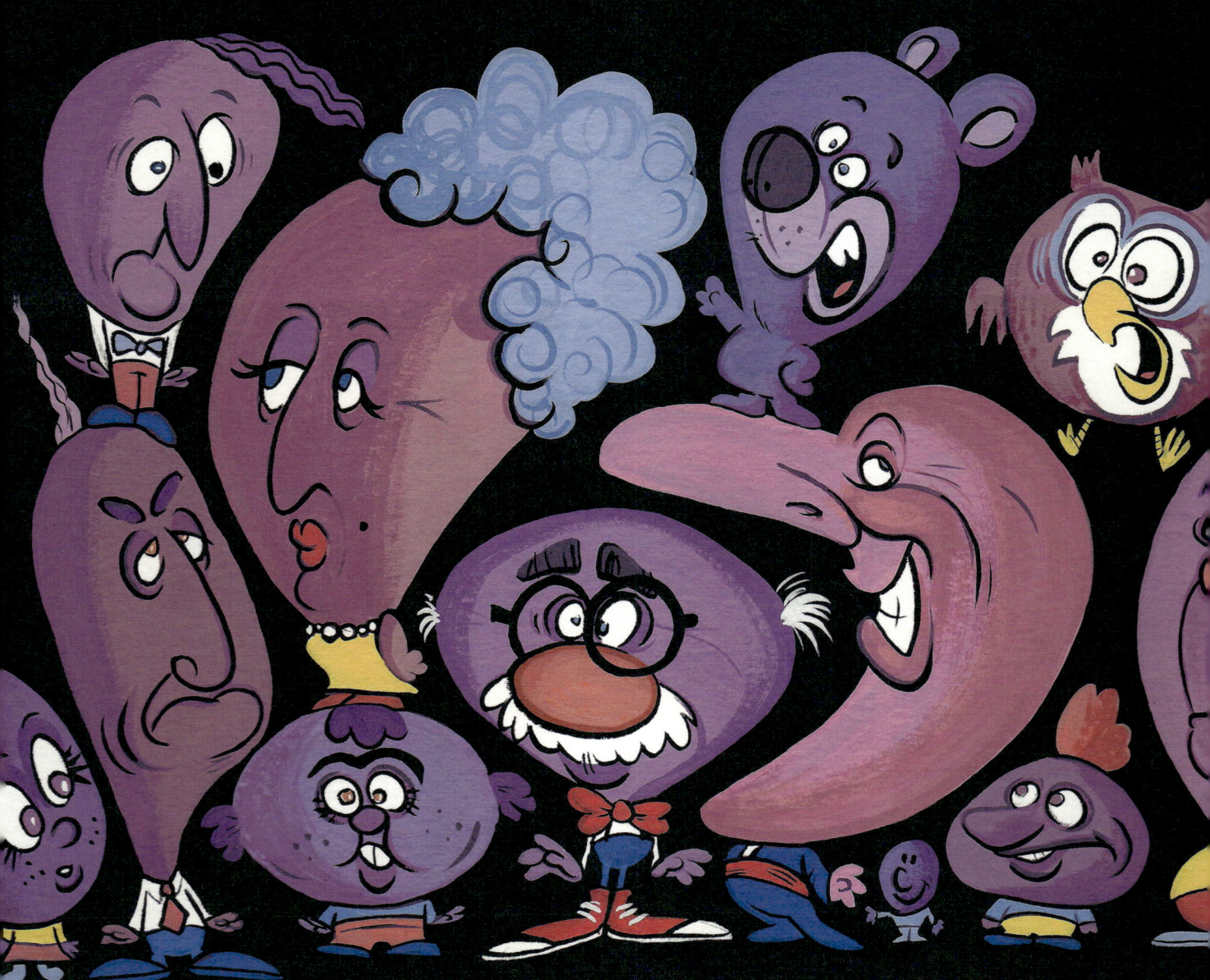

There is quite a crowd of us in Adam's head...

Did you know that people think about 70 thousand THOUGHTS each day? This is probably true on a regular day, however, on the eve of your birthday LEGIONS of our buddies come along.

When you're excited, worried or afraid it is our favourite time to pay a visit!

Are there any THOUGHTS in your mind right now?

CHECK AGAIN!

We come and go as we please
so you might sometimes think we are the boss.
But don't be fooled – **YOU ARE IN CHARGE**.
We are just guests.

We might seem real but we are not always true. So do watch out: we might trick you!

We can be **HUGE** and easy to notice.

We can be **STICKY** and insist on staying no matter what you do (even though you are trying to finish your homework!).

We can take you down STRANGE,
most unexpected paths.

We might try to **TAKE OVER**,
boss you around or even trap you...

...but you can always notice us and check what we are up to
– all you need to do is **PAUSE** and **PAY ATTENTION**.

Tonight, **THOUGHTS** are not leaving Adam alone - he's trying everything he can **THINK OF**.

He says: I watched a cartoon once where a sheep counted sheep to help it sleep. I figured that there was no harm giving it a go:

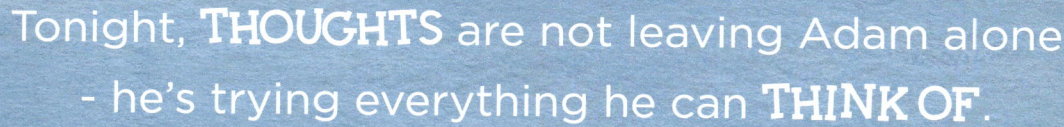

1, 2, 3, 4, 5, 6... this isn't working...
What number should I count to?

1, 2, 3... I won't wake up on time tomorrow and will be late for school. I've been late so many times, Ms. Kim will be mad...

Oh no, still awake...
I need to make sure my eyes are closed,
that's the problem. Close, don't open.
Don't open. **DO NOOOOOT!**
I feel dizzy, I'll open just a little.

What if no one shows up to my party? NO ONE came to Kate's party. Maybe because it was Halloween that day. My costume last year was awesome – a skeleton! Looked so real! Some costumes can be SCARY...

What was that? What's this noise?
Is there anyone there!?

MUM!!!!

"It is nothing, darling" Mum said having checked my room. "You can't sleep because your mind keeps **THINKING**. You need to **QUIET YOUR MIND**," she added. She kissed me goodnight, and left.

"Mum!!! My mind won't stop THINKING" I said!
"Now it is THINKING about thinking!"

Mum: Minds **THINK**, that's their job.

They remember, like when you have a **MEMORY** of the last holiday. They **PLAN**, when you **THINK** where you'll put your red balloons and they **WORRY** if any of your friends will come.

And right now you are **THINKING** that you can't sleep, which stops you from sleeping! **THOUGHTS** are very useful but can keep your mind busy.

"Does everyone's mind do that?" I asked.

Mum nodded and smiled. "So what do I do now?" I cried.

"Paying attention to the **BODY** helps settle the mind. Lie down comfortably." Mum said softly – "And close your eyes if you like. Notice your **THOUGHTS** in your mind right now. Let them **PASS**. They will stick if you try to push them away!"

Take 5 deep breaths –
in... out... in... out... in... out...

Remember to fully exhale, until there is no more air left in your belly...

Notice your **BODY** as it's breathing...

Notice your **FEET**. You can pretend they are illuminated by a soft, gentle glow. They might feel warm, cold, still, moving, tingling, numb, relaxed or something else. The glow is now slowly moving up towards your knees.

Notice your **KNEES**...

... the glow continues to travel up to your thighs (notice the feeling, soft, hard, still, moving, heavy or something else).

Up to the hips (if you like you can move a little to make it easier to notice), up to your tummy (is it moving as you breathe?), and chest (rising, falling, expanding, contracting, open, closed...).

If your mind starts **THINKING** (**THOUGHTS** love to turn up out of the blue, remember?) very gently bring your attention back to the body... Your shoulders are now surrounded by the glow, notice your shoulders and what they feel like right now. The warm glow moves up to your cheeks... And your eyes.

"Good night darling." Mum kissed my forehead.

"Get some rest busy mind, tomorrow there will be plenty for you to THINK about," was my last THOUGHT of the day.

Did you know that the skill of noticing and adjusting your THINKING, known as METACOGNITION, is an important one for people of all ages? Scientists found that METACOGNITION helps us learn, have better relationships with others and generally feel HAPPIER. The good news is that it can be developed through PRACTICE!

Try answering the following questions:

- Can you give an example of a THOUGHT you have noticed?
- Was the THOUGHT you noticed about the past, present or the future?
- What are you THINKING right now?
- How is this THOUGHT making you feel in your body?
- Are your THOUGHTS always true?
- What can you do if the THOUGHT you notice isn't helpful to you in the moment (for example makes it hard for you to focus on your reading)?

Made in the USA
Columbia, SC
07 December 2024